What Our Readers Have Said...

Applicability

"These books are great tools that should be used as guidelines for our everyday supervisory practices. You need to take the time to do a short self-evaluation when reading them."

•

"The things and problems we deal with everyday are discussed in these books."

•

Convenience

"I like this because I can take them with me to read at a convenient time. I feel the little time I have to spend in the office is best use on activities that directly relate to revenue opportunities. I like the short amount of time it takes to keep up with these."

•

"I just read each book, and then file it for future reference."

•

"I like the fact that the format allows the books to be reviewed as time permits. All work has been conducted on personal, evening/weekend time."

•

Challenge

"My thought is that the real value of these books comes into effect when doing the action plans."

•

"The challenge when I think a specific topic does not apply is to find a way to make it apply."

•

Clarity

"Short and sweet. These books are easy to comprehend."

•

"These books are very easy to read and clearly outlined."

•

"Easy to use, understand, and reference if needed."

•

Relevance

"I have enjoyed reading these books. They are relevant to today's work environment and the ongoing change in the way we manage our workforce."

•

"I believe the contents of the Pinpoint series are excellent. It causes one to reflect on the daily dynamics in working with oneself as well as with management and peers."

•

"I do feel that these books have been very helpful to me at my job."

•

"I do enjoy reading each of theses books and it gives some real thought to its instruction."

•

Establishing Trust & Credibility

Pinpoint Customer Service Skill Development Training Series

TIMOTHY F. BEDNARZ

MAJORIUM
BUSINESS PRESS

Pinpoint Customer Service Skill Development Training Series
"Establishing Trust & Credibility"
Timothy F. Bednarz

Graphic design: Monika Pawlak

Majorium Business Press
2025 Main Street
Stevens Point, WI 54481
715.342.1018 • 800.654.4935

ISBN 978-1-882181-40-7

Printed in the United States of America

Introduction

The Pinpoint Customer Service Skill Development Training Series is designed for targeted training and education regarding increased improvement in a specific skill or competency.

Each book within this series is designed to be easy to use, understand and apply to your job. It can be used as a basis for training individuals, as a discussion guide or as a personal training tool.

Each chapter within this book discusses a specific concept. When you have completed all eight chapters you should have a 360° perspective of the topic.

Additionally, each chapter is divided into specific sections:

- The first section provides you with an overview of the topic
- The Implications section discusses why the concept is important, and why it is important to learn and apply.
- The Strategies, Tips & Techniques to Apply section teaches how to use and apply the particular concept to your work.
- The Points to Ponder section gives you something to think about or to be discussed with a group setting. These are questions not meant to be immediately answered, but to be pondered over time.
- The Training Activity section provides you with the tools to transfer what you have learned to your job. It is designed to help create an action plan to effectively apply the concept.

Each of the topics in this series is time-tested and proven in the marketplace. They have been used by thousands of employees as training tools. Many of the users have commented that what made these books valuable, was the ability to refer to them when a problem surfaced. They indicated that they remembered reading about the exact problem. They referred back to these books and found an appropriate solution.

You will find them equally valuable as a resource in your professional development library.

Table of Contents

LEARNING OBJECTIVES:

- About the importance of trust and credibility.
- To understand how the customer views them.
- What it takes to establish trust and credibility.
- How to develop skills to work as a team to build customer trust.
- How their personal actions and attitudes affect the customer's trust in them.

1

Why Trust and Credibility Are Important

When a customer contacts a company, the service representative inherits a predetermined level of trust and confidence built upon the expectations a customer develops prior to purchasing the company's product or service. The service representative is the company, and how he or she responds determines the level of trust and confidence the customer leaves with.

IMPLICATIONS — WHAT THIS MEANS TO YOU

In many service environments, it is easy for customer service representatives to be overwhelmed by a challenging contact load of demanding and hostile customers. There may be a host of factors that are causing multiple problems for the service representative to handle. All can cause him or her to become terse and impatient with the customer, desensitized by hearing the same problem over and over again. Yet, to the customer, his or her problem is unique. Each feels that they have earned the right to voice a complaint and demand a solution.

This is important for service representatives to understand because customers who have invested their money in a product or service have trusted the company to stand behind its promises and bring a sense of confidence that their problems will be fixed in a timely and responsive manner. This is the implicit promise made with every purchase. It creates a specific expectation of a high quality of service. This is how a company is judged and that responsibility falls on the service representative's shoulders.

STRATEGIES, TIPS & TECHNIQUES TO APPLY

The concept of trust and credibility as related to the service representative is a complex one. When a customer buys a product or service from a company, they are forming a contract. In some instances, the customer signs a formal contract that defines the terms of the agreement. In other cases, when a product or service is purchased without a formal agreement, the contract is implicit or taken for granted. In both instances, when a customer makes a purchase in any form, they are taking a leap of faith. They are trusting that the product or service will perform as promised, whether in an advertisement or as represented by a salesperson. Additionally, they are trusting that the company will stand behind the products or services that they produce, so that if something does go wrong, the customer's money will be refunded or the product will be repaired or replaced. Finally, customers are trusting that the company's products or services will meet their perceptions of what they expect to receive. This contract is bound in the customer's mind when they pay for the purchase.

This relationship of perceived trust is brought to the service representative when a problem occurs or the customer has questions about the use and application of the product or service. From the customer's perspective, the moment of truth that they experience with the service representative should be an affirmation of the contract created when they purchased the company's product or service. Implicit in that contract is that the customer will receive quick and responsive service in a timely manner by a courteous service representative who makes him or her feel important and valued. Nothing is stated in the agreement that a perceived level of service will be provided. It is expected and implicit in the agreement with the customer. When customers encounter poor service or slow response times, they feel that the contract has been broken and that they have been betrayed by a shattered sense of trust. This results in a loss of confidence in the company and its promises and guarantees.

Conversely, when a problem occurs and the customer receives timely and responsive service to quickly resolve his or her problem, the initial commitment made by the company to guarantee its products and services is reinforced. The customer's level of confidence is heightened. This is precisely why customers who have problems that are quickly resolved have higher personal levels of customer loyalty. The company's promise was tested and the customer believes no matter what will happen, it will stand by him or her.

When customers deal with service representatives, they are bringing with them the trust and confidence established by the company. It is how the service representative manages his or her moment of truth with the customer that determines if that trust will be strengthened or violated. This is a big responsibility that most service representatives don't understand they have. They are literally the keepers of the promise made by the company to the customer. This is why their personal actions have an impact on a company's bottom line and long-term viability to survive.

POINTS TO PONDER — SOMETHING TO THINK ABOUT

1. Do you understand how you can personally strengthen or undermine a customer's confidence in your company?
2. Does that knowledge change or challenge your personal attitude toward your customers?

TRAINING ACTIVITY — APPLICATION & ACTION PLAN

1. Identify the factors that develop customer trust and confidence in your company's products and services.
2. Determine what levels of trust and confidence does a customer bring to the company.
3. Identify factors that enhance trust and confidence.
4. Identify the factors that undermine trust and confidence.
5. Determine how this creates a customer's perspective when contacting you.

2

Your Personal Integrity

Every customer contact is a moment of truth in the customer's eyes. It is how he or she judges and evaluates a company's performance in the light of an individual employee's behavior. The image and reputation of the company rests on the employee's shoulders and relies on his or her personal integrity.

IMPLICATIONS – WHAT THIS MEANS TO YOU

All relationships are built upon a foundation of trust. If the customer doesn't trust the company, he or she has no confidence that it will stand behind its products or services. The customer brings his or her trust and confidence to the relationship when contacting the company about a problem or with a question. This is a basic customer expectation.

This is important for service representatives to understand because their actions have the ability to build and sustain the trust or to violate it. This is what a moment of truth is ultimately about: keeping the trust with the customer. The personal integrity of the service representative is placed on the line with every contact because the customer is trusting him or her to do the right thing to resolve the problem or answer the question.

STRATEGIES, TIPS & TECHNIQUES TO APPLY

Many individuals in today's working environment take on a "winning at all costs" mentality. In their minds the ends justify the means, and if that means being dishonest or unethical in their personal and professional behaviors, so be it. Yet, with the recent high profile corporate scandals including Enron, Global Crossing and Arthur Andersen, the public is scrutinizing the behaviors exhibited by companies and their employees. Consequently, the winning at all costs attitude exhibited by many companies and eager managers is quickly falling into disrepute.

Service representatives may feel that because it is unlikely that a customer will talk with them more than once, they are justified or even comfortable with making dishonest and unethical statements. In many instances, they feel they will not be accountable for their actions and that it's the customer's problem. It takes on a "just do your job and tell them what they want to hear" attitude. The problem is that they are the company in the customer's eyes and what they say or do represents the company's viewpoint and procedures. While the individual service representative may duck personal accountability, the company does not. Its image and reputation are permanently tarnished by the words and actions of an uncaring and possibly dishonest employee.

During the 1930s a manager was employed by a Chicago bank to assume the management of a bankrupt aluminum pots and pans manufacturing company. The manager immediately noticed that there was an ethical problem with how customers were handled and the representations made to them. In response he created the "Four Way Test" to measure the actions of all employees and their relationships with all customers. The result of these actions was the creation of a highly ethical and responsive company that was able to work its way out of bankruptcy and ultimately make the manager a very rich individual. Upon his death, he left the copyright to the Four Way Test to Rotary International, which promotes it through its organization. It is an excellent ethical decision making tool that all employees should use in their daily activities.

THE FOUR WAY TEST

Of the things, we think say or do:

1. Is it the TRUTH?
2. Is it FAIR to all concerned?
3. Will it build GOODWILL and BETTER FRIENDSHIPS?
4. Will it be BENEFICIAL to all concerned?

It should be noted that this is a decision making tool. It does not tell one how to act or what he or she should do. But it does pose four questions that can be used to guide an individual's actions and the consequences of his or her decisions. It has a place in both the personal and professional lives of all individuals.

POINTS TO PONDER — SOMETHING TO THINK ABOUT

1. How ethical is your behavior when dealing with your customers?
2. Do you feel pressure to use unethical practices with your customers?

TRAINING ACTIVITY — APPLICATION & ACTION PLAN

Apply the FOUR WAY TEST to your personal and professional life for the next thirty days to make it a habit.

Of the things, we say or do

1. Is it the TRUTH?
2. Is it FAIR to all concerned?
3. Will it build GOOD WILL and BETTER FRIENDSHIPS?
4. Will it be BENEFICIAL to all concerned?

3

Trust Is Built Upon Credibility

The customer relationship is built on both stated and implicit trust that the company will stand behind its products and services as well as the promises they made prior to the sale. A number of factors come into play during the service relationship that either confirms the customer's confidence in the company or erodes its credibility.

IMPLICATIONS – WHAT THIS MEANS TO YOU

While the concept of customer trust and credibility can become rather complex, it is important for service representatives to understand their role and responsibilities in building and sustaining customer trust and credibility. Obviously unless the service representative's responsibilities include dealing with a consistent number of the same customers, it is difficult to build the relationship with an individual customer where trust becomes a factor. However, they should understand that their single interaction is part of the ongoing relationship with the customer where trust and credibility come into play. It is how they manage that individual moment of truth that can determine if trust and credibility is sustained and maintained in the customer's mind.

STRATEGIES, TIPS & TECHNIQUES TO APPLY

When interacting with a customer service representative, the customer will gauge the credibility of his or her actions based upon several criteria. While the customer may not be consciously evaluating each and every factor, the sum total of the responses will determine the overall credibility of the moment of truth in the customer's mind. These factors include:

Reasonableness of the Response

Every customer brings an expectation of how his or her problem should be resolved by the company they are dealing with. As the price and complexity of the product or service increases so will the customer's expectations. Consequently, when dealing with a customer service representative, the first thing the customer will be evaluating is the reasonableness of the response in comparison to their expectations. For example, if the customer expected an immediate replacement of a defective product and is told that they will have to ship the product to a warranty center and wait four to six weeks, they may consider that to be an unreasonable response. That solution doesn't solve the problem. It delays the solution for an unacceptable time period with a vague result or outcome.

Timeliness

While research has demonstrated that customers can accept that fact the problems do occur, they do expect them to be fixed quickly and without additional problems or hassles. When they encounter what they judge to be unrealistic and unacceptable delays, this harms the credibility of the company. They were promised when they made the purchase of a product or service that it would work and perform to a certain standard. When that product fails to do so, they expect either a timely repair or replacement. When the company fails to stand behind this implicit promise, the trust between the company and the customer is broken.

Attitude and Demeanor of the Service Representative

Customers feel they have the right to be treated with respect and courtesy. If the example cited earlier is used where the customer is informed that their product will not be fixed in a timely fashion and the service representative demonstrates an uncaring or unconcerned attitude about the customer's problem, then the issue is further complicated.

However, if the service representative displays an empathic tone and carefully explains step-by-step what will happen, it is more likely the customer may be soothed and calmed. While the outcome may still be considered unreasonable, the credibility is either maintained or restored. How the service representative approaches and handles a potentially sticky problem will determine its ultimate outcome.

Representations of the Company

The representations of the company before the sale and its stated and implicit promises made to the customer are a critical part of the credibility equation. If representations were made concerning future and potential problems and the level of service to be delivered, these will come into play. If the example of the customer being informed that it will take approximately four to six weeks to have the problem resolved is followed and he or she was told that immediate replacement would be made prior to the sale, then a problem exists that conflicts with the company's policy. Not only is the response unreasonable to the customer, it is not what was represented to him or her. The credibility is instantly lost because the customer feels he or she was lied to.

Expectations of the Customer

The expectations of the customer are the yardstick by which credibility is measured. The service representative or any other representative of the company cannot gauge it. Perceptions were created that formed specific expectations. Rightly or wrongly, it is these specific expectations that will determine the credibility of the moment of truth and of the company.

POINTS TO PONDER — SOMETHING TO THINK ABOUT

1. Do you understand how your personal actions have the power to change a customer's perspectives and expectations?
2. Do you comprehend the factors that impact the company's credibility with a customer?

TRAINING ACTIVITY — APPLICATION & ACTION PLAN

1. On a sheet of paper, compare and contrast your perspectives and viewpoints of the following factors versus the customer's expectations:
    - Reasonableness of the Response
    - Timeliness
    - Attitude and Demeanor of the Service Representative
    - Representations of the Company
    - Expectations of the Customer
2. Determine how does your perspective differ from the customer's.
3. Identify the specific differences.
4. Determine if the customer's expectations are realistic.
5. Identify personal actions you can take to meet the customer's expectations.

4

Does the Customer Have Any Reason to Believe You?

There are customers who have been promised solutions to their problems, only never to receive them or when they do, find that they don't work. They feel the company has failed to stand behind its promises and that it cannot be believed or trusted.

IMPLICATIONS – WHAT THIS MEANS TO YOU

Many customers who contact a company and talk with a service representative are hostile and angry over how they were previously treated or because their problem wasn't solved. In many service environments, uncaring and unconcerned service representatives will pass the customer along without taking the time and action to fix the problem.

This is important for service representatives to understand because it does not take much to be a "service star" – the one individual who takes responsibility for the customer's problem until it is either fixed or eliminated. They take the time and demonstrate the concern to customers that their business is important and that they are committed to their satisfaction.

STRATEGIES, TIPS & TECHNIQUES TO APPLY

A common dilemma that many service representatives encounter is when a frustrated customer contacts them and doesn't trust or believe what they have to say. This can be typically traced back to the following problems and issues:

Duration or Repetition of the Problem

Research has repeatedly demonstrated that the faster the problem is solved, the happier and more loyal a customer will be. On the flip side of that finding is the customer who is experiencing a problem that remains unresolved for a long duration of time or is recurring. The customer, not the service representative, defines what constitutes "long." This will depend on the size and initial cost of the purchase. However, if a reasonable amount of time has passed without resolution, the trust between the company and the customer is broken. At this point, the credibility of anything said to them will not exist.

The solution is for the service representative to get the problem immediately fixed or eliminated. If they are not empowered to do so, then the problem should be personally referred to someone who can, with the service representative maintaining control of the situation until the customer is satisfied.

Prior Promises

The customer has repeatedly called and been promised a solution that has not materialized. The promises have remained unfulfilled for a variety of legitimate reasons, but the customer perceives that the company is lying to him or her.

The solution is identical to the one in the prior problem with a minor twist. The service representative should follow up with both the company's internal support staff to ensure that the promised solution is fulfilled and the customer to inform him or her of every step of the solution. This will reestablish both trust and confidence in the customer's mind.

Ineffective Solutions

The solutions to the customer's problem either haven't worked or are ineffective. The problem remains unsolved and has been complicated by any prior attempts to correct it. This results in a loss of customer confidence in the company and its products and services.

The solution is for the service representative to forward the problem to the proper technical department to either resolve the issue immediately replace the product or service. The service representative should remain involved with the situation following up with the internal support team and customer until the problem is fixed and the customer is satisfied.

Rigid Policies and Procedures

The customer is frustrated because other company representatives have hidden behind rigid and inflexible policies and procedures that have thwarted the customer's ability to resolve the problem. This results in the customer not believing that the company is willing to fix the problem. He or she feels used and stuck with a defective product or service.

The solution is for the service representative to take steps to fix the problem if he or she is empowered or to refer the problem to a supervisor or manager who does have the authority. When referring the customer to a superior the representative should have confidence that the customer will be handled properly and have his or her problem resolved.

Perception the Company Doesn't Care

In many cases, the customer has experienced a series of problems and broken promises. They feel helpless and that no one in the company cares about him or her. The system has completely broken down and failed the customer.

The solution is for the service representative to take complete charge and to immediately take the necessary steps to assist the customer and assure that their satisfaction is attained. Often, the customer feels this way because they have been passed from one party to another. It will take a single person taking charge of the situation and ensuring that the customer receives the service he or she is entitled to until the problem is fixed.

Customer Frustration and Anxiety

There are customers who have made countless calls and been passed from person-to-person without having their problem solved. They have reached the end of their rope and they are angry and hostile.

The service representative should allow the customer to vent in these circumstances, taking notes of his or her experience to pass along to management. Once the customer has cooled down, the service representative should take charge and make sure that the problem is immediately solved. Additionally, the service representative should follow up with the customer to make sure everything was resolved to his or her satisfaction.

Irrational Customer

There are customers who are irrational and demanding. Nothing that can be done will personally satisfy their demands. They are belligerent and demeaning in their remarks and comments.

In these situations, the service representative should politely refer these individuals to a supervisor and allow him or her to deal with the customer.

POINTS TO PONDER – SOMETHING TO THINK ABOUT

1. How often do you encounter customers who feel that they can't believe or trust what you are telling them?
2. What is the most common cause of this problem in your company's service environment?

TRAINING ACTIVITY – APPLICATION & ACTION PLAN

Define what it takes to be a "service star" in your company.

1. Define what extra steps or actions can you take.
2. Determine what you are empowered to do in behalf of the customer.
3. Identify reliable individuals you can refer customers to who you know will make sure the problem will get fixed.
4. Identify the unreliable individuals who you want to avoid when problems occur.
5. Identify what other actions you can take that will ensure satisfaction that are above and beyond your job's expectations.

5

How Personal Actions Affect Your Credibility

While many service situations are beyond the control service representatives, how they behave during a customer contact does affect their personal credibility with the customer. This contributes to the overall image, reputation and credibility of the company.

IMPLICATIONS – WHAT THIS MEANS TO YOU

Many customer service encounters go beyond being professional and business like. Service representatives come across as acting brisk, detached, uncaring and impersonal. Some are arrogant and condescending. Yet, these actions and behaviors serve only to undermine trust and credibility rather than to build and reinforce it.

This is important for service representatives to understand because while the customer can bring anger and perceptions of mistrust and lack of confidence to the discussion, their individual actions can either reinforce or dispel these notions. As a reality check, service representatives should ask themselves if they treat their customers in the same manner that they wish to be treated?

STRATEGIES, TIPS & TECHNIQUES TO APPLY

Undoubtedly, the actions and behaviors of the individual service representative impact his or her credibility with the customer. They set the tone for the customer's experience and define his or her moment of truth. These are defined by the following:

Personality

The personality of the service representative sets an immediate tone for the conversation. A helpful and positive attitude will dispel anger and hostility, while a defensive and abrupt attitude invites confrontation and belligerence.

Listening

Service representatives must be effective listeners. They should know when to allow the customer to vent his or her frustrations and how to ask questions that determine the cause of the problem. Only then is the service representative in a position to be helpful and of service to the customer.

Effective listening and questioning skills allow service representatives to assist the customer in both defining and clarifying the problem. It allows them to probe to understand the seriousness and immediacy and what steps they need to take to fix or eliminate it.

Personal Attitude

The service representative's personal attitude strongly affects his or her credibility with the customer. The service representative with a "servant mentality" will telegraph to customers a lack of concern, and act like they are an interruption or disruption in the representative's life. On the other hand, the service representative with a "service attitude" communicates that the customer and the problem are welcome and provide an opportunity to serve him or her. The subtleties of personal attitude are not lost on customers. They are communicated very clearly.

Empathy

It is easy for service representatives to become desensitized to customer problems since they tend to repeatedly hear the same problem over and over again. However, to the customer the problem is real and serious. It is causing his or her discomfort and inconvenience.

How service representatives personally respond to the customer and his or her problem affects their credibility. If the service representative is unconcerned, it communicates a message that he or she doesn't care about the customer. If the service representative empathizes with the customer, he or she feels valued and important. This builds trust and rapport that is required to effectively be of service.

Attention to Detail

When service representatives demonstrate attention to the small details, it communicates a message that this individual really cares about the customer's problem. It is reassuring and builds and fosters both trust and credibility.

Personal Responsibility

Service representatives should not minimize the impact that personal responsibility has on the customer. When they assure the customer that they will take charge of the problem until it is fixed, this underscores and reinforces trust and credibility. In too many service situations, customers experience service representatives who pass the problem on to another individual without making sure it is fixed. They are impersonal and uncaring. This erodes trust and credibility and often only complicates the problem further.

Undoubtedly many service-related problems can be resolved or eliminated if service representatives took personal responsibility to fix the customer's problem in the first place. Many problems are only complicated when the issue is passed from individual to individual without the appropriate action ever being taken.

Personal Follow-Up

While it's a minor point and may not be necessary with every customer contact, following up with difficult problems or frustrated customers can go a long way to restore trust and credibility. It communicates a simple message of care and concern, which may not be immediately appreciated, but will always be remembered.

POINTS TO PONDER – SOMETHING TO THINK ABOUT

1. Have you considered how your personal actions affect your credibility?
2. Have you experienced credibility problems because of your personal actions and behaviors with a customer?

TRAINING ACTIVITY – APPLICATION & ACTION PLAN

Determine how you can take charge of a customer's problem and take "personal responsibility" for it.

1. Identify the parameters or limits of the actions that you are empowered to take in the customer's behalf.
2. Determine how far you typically go within those parameters for the customer.
3. Define how you can specifically take charge of a customer's problem.
    - What can you do and how can you do it?
4. Identify the specific actions that you can take in the customer's behalf.
    - What can you do and how can you do it?

6

Trust: Building It in Small Steps

Every time customers walk away from a contact with a company feeling good about how they were treated and satisfied with the solution, their confidence in that company rises. A trust is established and is reaffirmed in the customer's mind.

IMPLICATIONS — WHAT THIS MEANS TO YOU

Every customer contact is a moment of truth for a company because each has the potential of either strengthening customer confidence or trust or destroying it entirely. The company is therefore on the line every time there is a customer contact. However, carefully managed moments of truth result in the incremental building of customer trust and confidence in small but expanding steps.

This is important for service representatives to understand because many feel their job isn't important or that they are not paid well enough to care about their customers. As companies struggle to survive in an increasingly competitive world, customer service takes on an increasingly important role in customer retention. How an individual service representative acts and performs does have important ramifications on a company's success. Service representatives should not minimize their importance to both the customer and the company.

STRATEGIES, TIPS & TECHNIQUES TO APPLY

Customer service environments vary in their levels of interaction with the customer. In the business-to-consumer environment, the service representative may come into contact with multiple customers, but rarely the same one more than once. In the business-to-business service environment, the customer contact can be sporadic or continuous. Each has specific implications to the development of trust in the service environment. In the singular contact environment, the customer is basing their trust in the company and its representatives, whereas in the service environment where representatives have ongoing contact, the levels of trust become more personal as the customer and representative develop bonds of trust and rapport. In all instances, every moment of truth and customer contact is an opportunity for the company through its service representatives to build and strengthen the bonds of trust, whether it is through a single or sporadic contact or an ongoing relationship. In all instances, the following expectations need to be met if trust is to be developed and nurtured.

Speed

While research has shown that the faster a problem is solved, the more loyal a customer becomes, there is an additional element of speed that needs to be considered. That is the speed of the response. This may include the time it takes to respond to a customer inquiry via email or phone. The faster a company is able to respond to a customer inquiry, the stronger the customer's trust will be. This is not about the time needed to resolve the customer's problem, but the time required to respond to the initial inquiry.

Accuracy

An additional element that strengthens customer confidence and trust is the accuracy of the response. This means that the information and answers provided to the customer are factually accurate and will help the customer resolve his or her problem. Inaccurate information means that the customer will have to contact the company an additional time to clarify and get the right information. This diminishes the customer's confidence and trust in the company.

Competence

One area that is a "trustbuster" with customers is the level of competence they witness in their dealings with a company. A well-trained and knowledgeable service representative creates a strong sense of customer confidence that he or she will be taken care of. The service representative that doesn't know the answer or where to refer the customer, to handle his or her problem creates worry and anxiety. The customer feels that no one knows what is doing on and that his or her problems will not be handled and resolved in a competent manner.

Reliability

Customers have specific expectations that what they are told the company will do will actually happen with some degree of accuracy. If a billing problem occurs and the customer is told a credit will be issued to him or her, they have a reasonable expectation that it will happen. When it doesn't happen within a reasonable amount of time, the customer's confidence and trust is diminished because they are forced to go through the procedure again, only now it is more complicated by the lack of action on the company's part.

Courtesy

Customers are people and they have the expectation of being treated in a courteous and professional manner. Many problems are further complicated by rude and condescending service representatives who make the customer feel minimized and unimportant. This is destructive to any confidence and trust the customer may have. The service representative may be right and have won the battle, but in the end his or her actions can cost the company a customer.

POINTS TO PONDER — SOMETHING TO THINK ABOUT

1. How do you see trust develop in your customers?
2. What steps can you take to increase customer trust?

TRAINING ACTIVITY — APPLICATION & ACTION PLAN

1. Determine what defines accuracy in the customer's mind.
2. Identify what steps you can take to increase the levels of accuracy that you can provide.
3. Determine how you can measure your accuracy.
4. Keep records and determine how much your accuracy has increased over time.

7

Re-establishing Lost Trust and Credibility

Research has shown that the majority of customers who have lost their confidence in a company simply walk away. The customer that is taking the time to voice their complaints is providing the company with an opportunity to win this individual back.

IMPLICATIONS – WHAT THIS MEANS TO YOU

When customers have lost their confidence in a company, somewhere along the way the bonds of trust and credibility have been broken between them. For some reason the customer feels that the company has failed to stand behind its promises. This may be caused by the company's business practices, how the customer was treated or by the company's failure to resolve the problem to the customer's satisfaction.

This is important for service representatives to understand because unless they are directly involved in the problem or their actions resulted in the customer's dissatisfaction, most problems are the result of circumstances out of their control. However, their role and responsibility in the company dictates that they are the point person to handle the problem.

STRATEGIES, TIPS & TECHNIQUES TO APPLY

When customers have reached the point that they no longer trust a company and what the company says no longer is credible, the service representative has a difficult task ahead of him or her. Something serious has severed the relationship, and the service representative must take action to reconnect the customer. Some recommended steps include:

Be Professional

Service representatives must remain professional through the entire situation. Chances are the customer will be angry, hostile and emotional, and it's easy to lower oneself to that level. Service representatives must resist this urge and handle themselves in a competent manner.

Additionally, unless they have caused the problem, service representatives should understand that the customer is angry at the company and not with them personally. They cannot take comments and remarks personally.

Be Patient

Service representatives must be patient with the customer. When customers become enraged and emotional, their comments and remarks will seem to be rambling and hard to follow. In many cases the customer will voice the inconvenience and potential damage the problem has caused him or her. The service representative must empathize with the customer and win their confidence. This is an important first step.

Let the Customer Vent Frustrations

It is important for service representatives to allow the customer to vent their frustrations and emotions. Until this negative energy is dissipated, the conversation will not move forward. It will be a replay of the same feelings and events.

Define the Problem

Service representatives should immediately begin to define the problem by getting the customer to give the facts behind the situation. If this information is already on file in the customer's account, the service representative should review and clarify what exactly has occurred.

In this situation, it is important for service representatives to separate facts from opinion and feelings. It is necessary to deal with the objective actions of the company that has created the problem.

Define What Happened

Once the problem is adequately defined, the service representative must find out what exactly happened and if anything the company and its representatives have done contributed to the problem. They must separate the "what should have been done" from the "what actually was done." This will assist them in determining what actions need to be done to resolve the problem.

Determine Reasonableness of Demands

The customer will have demands and expectations of what they want the company to do to resolve the problem. Research has shown that if the customer is specifically asked what it would take to solve the problem, his or her expectations are often lower than what the company is prepared to offer.

Undoubtedly there are circumstances where the customer's demands are both frivolous and unreasonable. In these circumstances, the service representative can explain the options that they are authorized to provide to the customer. If the customer remains adamant in their demands, the service representative may be required to refer the customer to their supervisor or manager for further evaluation and action.

Take Immediate Action

Once a resolution is arrived at, the service representative should immediately implement it and follow up with all internal sources to ensure that it is put into immediate effect.

Follow Up

The service representative should follow up with the customer at every step to make sure what was agreed to is received within the promised time period. The customer should be queried as to their satisfaction.

It should be noted if the problem requires multiple calls, the customer service representative should be proactive in their communication. They should be always contacting the customer and not waiting for the customer to contact him or her. This activity rebuilds trust and reestablishes credibility. Additionally, it is important that the service representative does whatever is promised to the customer. This also rebuilds trust and reestablishes credibility.

POINTS TO PONDER – SOMETHING TO THINK ABOUT

1. What have been your personal experiences with customers that have lost their confidence in your company?
2. What techniques were you able to use to recover these customers?

TRAINING ACTIVITY – APPLICATION & ACTION PLAN

On a sheet of paper list ten possible factors that could result in broken trust with a customer.

1. Prioritize them in order of potential problems starting with the worst factor.
2. Identify the reasons the factors break the customer's trust.
3. Determine what you can do to re-establish the customer's trust.
4. Discuss your findings with your manager or supervisor for review to determine if these factors can be eliminated.

8

Do Not Hide Behind the Policy Manual

One thing that can destroy a service representative's credibility faster than anything else is when he or she chooses or is forced to hide behind company policy. When customers have a problem, it infuriates them and only makes matters worse when company policy is cited as the reason for not being able to do anything to help solve specific concerns.

IMPLICATIONS – WHAT THIS MEANS TO YOU

No individual company is free of problems and mistakes. However, a delayed resolution or a lack of a resolution based upon a company policy will quickly turn a customer into an activist. Activists are individuals who will do anything to spread the word of their poor experience to anyone who will listen. These are individuals, angered by their poor experiences, who will actively work against the interests of a company. They will do anything in their power to smear a company's reputation.

Most unhappy customers tell an average of 25 people of their negative experience. Activists will tell far more people, and, depending upon their influence, have the definite potential to drastically harm a company's business, image and reputation.

This is important for service representatives to understand and grasp because most customers view company policies as a ruse for not wanting to solve their problem. They expect service representatives to fight for them and to resolve their problem. They want some flexibility applied to arriving at a viable and acceptable solution.

Service representatives may win the battle when they rigidly apply company policies, but they will lose the war and the customer.

STRATEGIES, TIPS & TECHNIQUES TO APPLY

Most individuals are reasonable. When a problem occurs, they just want it fixed. Most understand that problems happen and they can live with that. However, when a problem does occur, they do expect a quick and timely resolution. The last thing they want is a bureaucratic service representative who refuses to resolve their individual problem and resorts to hiding behind the company handbook.

Customer relationships are built on trust. That means when there is a problem, the company and its representatives will quickly solve it. If a company has established sufficient trust to obtain a customer's business, it has also established an expectation in the customer's mind that it will always be there to make sure everything goes smoothly during times of trouble.

The problem occurs when a company has firm policies in place. Many policies are initially established to prevent the company from being taken advantage of by unscrupulous customers. But most companies do remain flexible if reasonable solutions are mutually agreed to when a problem does occur. Many are discovering the world is entirely too competitive to handle customers in a cavalier fashion.

The next time a customer problem occurs, service representatives should try this approach: "Our policy is not to issue a refund after 30 days. However, it's also our policy not to have unhappy customers. What do you consider to be a fair solution to this problem?"

When service representatives use this approach, they have a starting point for creating a satisfied, happy customer. It demonstrates that the service representatives care and are willing to listen and act to resolve the problem. This approach moves the process forward to solve the problem while keeping the customer content and loyal.

Great customer relationships are based upon trust and personal credibility. Customers expect service representatives to fight for them and make sure their problems are quickly resolved. Hiding behind a policy book only undermines and destroys a service representative's credibility. It makes it difficult for a company to ever regain a customer's confidence, loyalty and trust once this situation occurs.

POINTS TO PONDER — SOMETHING TO THINK ABOUT

1. How do you resolve a customer's problem when faced with a firm company policy that ties your hands? Explain.
2. How do you attempt to retain a customer who is infuriated by a company policy that is out of your control? Explain.

TRAINING ACTIVITY — APPLICATION & ACTION PLAN

Take a few minutes to view your company from the customer's perspective. Does your company have rules and policies that have caused customer problems because they feel some are unreasonable?

1. Identify and pinpoint problem areas.
2. Develop some alternative service strategies to minimize recurring problems and discuss them with your supervisor for implementation.

About the Author

Timothy F. Bednarz, Ph.D. is CEO of the American Management Development Group, Inc. For over 20 years he has researched, designed and authored hundreds of learning and development programs used by Fortune 1000 companies.

He is also the author of *Great! What Makes Leaders Great. What They Did, How They Did It and What You Can Learn from It* (2011).

Speaking Availability

Timothy F. Bednarz, Ph.D. is available for speaking engagements for your next meeting or association event. He can be contacted at 800-654-4935 or by e-mail at timothy.bednarz@majorium.com.

Bulk Sales

Bulk sales of this book or any other titles available from Majorium Business Press. Inquiries can be directed to sales@majorium.com, or by phone at 800-6654-4935.

Quick Order Form

Fax orders: 715-342-1118. Send this form.

Telephone orders: Call 800-654-4935 toll-free. Have your credit card ready.

Email orders: sales@majorium.com

Postal orders: Majorium Business Press, 2025 Main Street, Stevens Point, WI 54481, USA.

Please send the following books:

____

____

____

____

Please send more FREE information on:

❑Catalog ❑Speaking/Seminars ❑Mailing Lists ❑Consulting

Name: ____

Address: ____

City: ______________________________ State: ______ Zip: __________

Telephone: ____

Email address: ____

Sales tax: Please add 5.5% for products shipped to Wisconsin addresses.

Shipping by air:

United States: $4.00 for first book and $2.00 for each additional product.

International: $9.00 for first book; $5.00 for each additional product (estimate).

Made in the USA
Monee, IL
08 November 2026

67380783R00026